DECLUTTER YOUR HOME

The Simple Guide to Tidying and Cleaning Your Home, Room by Room

CONTENTS

- **INTRODUCTION** 3
- **CHAPTER ONE: UNDERSTANDING THE CONCEPT OF DECLUTTERING** 5
  - WHY LESS IS MORE 5
  - MINIMALISM vs. CONSUMERISM 7
  - WARNING SIGNS THAT YOU NEED TO DECLUTTER YOUR HOME 7
  - BENEFITS OF DECLUTTERING 9
- **CHAPTER TWO: THE MINDSET FOR DECLUTTERING** 11
  - DAILY HABITS TO DEVELOP TO HELP YOU WITH YOUR DECLUTTERING 11
  - LEARNING GRATITUDE AND MINDFULNESS FOR MINIMALISM 13
  - BEFORE YOU MAKE ANOTHER PURCHASE, ASK YOURSELF THESE VITAL QUESTIONS 14
- **CHAPTER THREE: THE BASICS OF DECLUTTERING** 17
- **CHAPTER FOUR: DEALING WITH KITCHEN** 23
  - WHERE TO BEGIN IN THE KITCHEN 23
  - KITCHEN APPLIANCES AND GADGETS 24
- **CHAPTER FIVE: THE MASTER BEDROOM** 29
  - STARTING UP 30
  - THE BEDROOM SURFACES 31
  - THE DRAWERS 31
  - DEMARCATING THE WORKSPACE FROM A RELAXATION SPACE 32
  - THE CLOSET 33
  - THE CHILDREN'S ROOM 34
- **CHAPTER SIX: DECLUTTERING THE HOME OFFICE** 36
  - THE MAJOR REQUIREMENT 36
  - STARTING UP THE PROCESS 37
  - THE PAPER CLUTTER 37
  - THE OFFICE DESK 38
  - THE BEST HABITS TO ADOPT TO PREVENT THE RE-ACCUMULATION OF PAPER CLUTTER 38
  - THE SCANNING OPTION 39
  - HANDLING THE DIGITAL CLUTTER IN YOUR WORKSPACE 40
  - ELECTRONICS AND CABLES 41
- **CHAPTER SEVEN: DECLUTTERING YOUR SCHEDULE** 43
- **CONCLUSION** 47

INTRODUCTION

The world we live in today has drastically failed us. Many of us have been made to believe that having more equates to being more. In fact, we've been conditioned to accept a pseudo-fact that our material possessions define who we are. But that's wrong on so many levels. Instead, we should learn to look above and beyond that mentality since less can often mean more. Less produces more happiness, more comfort, more space and ultimately more peace.

Specifically, many items that we come across everyday seem to point to the fact that our lives will turn out better if only we decide to buy a particular product. This is one reason that the advertisement industry is one of the wealthiest and most lucrative. The power to convince and confuse people to crowd their homes and lives with things they might not need is a common but manipulative skill in this modern age.

Before you begin the decluttering process, it's best that you understand and see reasons why you should join in this movement. Take a look around your home and observe all of the stuff and possessions that have filled up all the spaces. See the things you may have inherited, the belongings you may have bought. How many of those do you really need? How many of those are you still holding on to because of sentiments? Most of these items are things that gradually build up into clutter in your home? Sometimes you may return home and wish that they'd just disappear and leave you some space to breathe in fresh air. Unfortunately, no one is ever going to help you, so you must declutter your home by yourself.

This is why this book has been designed specifically with the aim of helping you to perform your own decluttering process. In the following chapters you'll be given actionable tips that will help you stay ahead of clutter and ultimately overcome it in your home. One suggestion to understand is that clutter is a weed that never wants to die. . It's always up and active, looking for a space to bring up its head and reclaim your home. That's why you'll need to be proactive in this fight against clutter. The clutter battle is one that people tend to ignore, not because they love its accumulation, but because they typically have no idea how to deal with it proactively. With this book, that problem is solved.

The approach that will be outlined in the following chapters is a simple and straightforward one. The actionable steps will help you t with the process of organizing and reclaiming the space in your home. But remember that it isn't all about the reading of the rules, but by its application. You can never see success in your decluttering venture if you don't begin to apply the principles here as soon as possible. Take this book as a daily guide through your decluttering process. You don't have to rush. For some people, decluttering can take only a few weeks. For others, a whole month isn't enough. Another set is comfortable with the procedure being as long as one year. The most important tip is that you remain consistent with your actions.

CHAPTER ONE: UNDERSTANDING THE CONCEPT OF DECLUTTERING

The concept of decluttering is often interchanged or confused to mean the same premise as organizing. However, these two concepts are distinct from each other. Decluttering mainly pertains to getting rid of the excesses in your home while organizing basically involves putting items in their places. Organizing is a sub-concept of decluttering.

To begin the decluttering process, one must first understand what can be classified as clutter so that you know what you're inspecting in your home. Clutter refers to anything that can cause disorganization, chaos, confusion, disorderliness or untidiness. If you take a look around your home, you'll be able to identify some stuff which can be classified as clutter, stuff that you barely use but still keep. For example, your skateboard from high school that you haven't used since you bought your car seven years ago. Or the flower vase your grandmother gave you as a birthday gift after her return from that vacation in Italy when you were a kid. All of these soon turn out to be unnecessary and begin to occupy space in your home. Sorting them out and removing them from your home is what is referred to as decluttering.

Clutter can form in your home as a result of varying factors such as excessive hoarding, materialism, impulsive buying or other sentimental reasons. These are some of the factors that you'll have to assess to effectively overcome the clutter in your home. Begin to adopt the 'Less is more' approach to life and reap the wholesome benefits of doing this.

WHY LESS IS MORE
To begin to declutter and accept the challenge is to first understand that less is more. The truth of that statement still exists even with how ironic it sounds.

For a greater part of our lives, we're burdened with the weight of owning and taking care of possessions. As younger children it wasn't always this way. All we cared about were toys. But as we grew older, we became more obsessed with stuff: the latest magazines, the biggest shoe brands and most expensive gadgets in this market. While these make our lives better in some ways, they should never become the anchor on which we cling to existence. Unfortunately, it's human nature to want to multiply possessions.

The less is more concept applies to more aspects of our lives than we can imagine. That phrase seems so simple at first glance; but on closer inspection, one will notice how powerful it is. The less is more concept is one that strives to battle the materialistic concept that has taken over our world today. Materialism leads to the buildup of clutter;

and if nothing is done about it, anxiety and stress become the order of the day. Here are main reasons why less is always more:

1. **Having less means having more space**

People love to live with enough space around them. The benefits of spaciousness are enormous. First, it offers healthy benefits since your lungs are blessed with fresh air. Then is the simple fact of your home being free from the invasion of pests and rodents who love to hide in stuffed corners of your home. When clutter builds up in your home, it covers up these spaces and leaves you feeling like an alien in your home. Dealing with clutter will help you to create more space and place you in charge as the owner of your home. There are many items in your home that are unneeded but yet occupying precious space that could have been used for something better. Conditioning yourself to live with less would have saved the stress right from the start.

2. **Having less helps you focus on things of value**

The act of decluttering does not essentially mean that you do away with everything you have. Instead, it's a concept that helps to build your focus and assist you to keep this focus on things that would add more value to your live. When we begin to jam-pack our lives with activities and possessions, it becomes quite easy to entertain carelessness and start chasing pavements. Decluttering will help you to reassess your life and values and settle for those things that are worthy of your time and attention. The ultimate benefit of this is the ability to do more, to achieve more, and become a better person in general.

3. **Having less provides you with mental clarity**

The more you own, the more you think. Being wealthy and having properties is all fun and games until it's time to manage all of this wealth. First, you'll need a personal assistant to keep track of all your possessions. That means more expenses to pay and one more person to worry about when you're budgeting. It's almost like a full cycle where an addition will lead to the need of another addition. No one is saying that you shouldn't grow, but take out time to remove the excesses even as you grow. Having less will help you easily keep stock of all you have and give them all your attention until you achieve success. Don't become a jack of all trade and master of none. You'll only end up stressing your mind.

4. **A Mind full of Gratitude**

If there's one virtue that decluttering helps you breed, it's the virtue of gratitude and contentment. The human nature is one that always seeks to acquire more, to get more and to own more. Sometimes this can lead to an excessive lust for wealth and can make an individual become selfish while thinking that his acquisitions will provide him with ultimate happiness. Happiness goes beyond the things that you acquire. It's a deeper concept that you can tap into when decluttering and minimalism is practiced. You'll then learn to live life for the present and not live in anxiety of the future.

MINIMALISM vs. CONSUMERISM

Before you begin your decluttering process, there are some concepts to clearly understand, so that you don't fall back into the clutter trap.

First off, minimalism is a concept that closely relates to decluttering. Let me put it this way: you can't achieve a minimalist lifestyle without first decluttering. Minimalism is the end product of decluttering, that point when your life has been purged of everything unnecessary.

Consumerism, on the other hand, is a notion that seeks to abolish the presence of minimalism in your life. While minimalism will tell you to think before you buy, consumerism will advise you to hastily buy before you think. Minimalism will ask you to be content with what you have, but consumerism will tell you to add more possessions because your possessions are the things that define you.

Unfortunately, we live in a world that leans more towards the consumerism angle of life. While going through your decluttering journey, you'll come across friends and relatives who will try to talk you out of it and tell you why your decision is the wrong one. It's going to be like a constant battle between good and evil in your mind, so I urge you to be prepared so you don't drop out and give up along the way.

WARNING SIGNS THAT YOU NEED TO DECLUTTER YOUR HOME

To prepare you for your decluttering process, you need to be able to identify some obvious signs in your home that show you that decluttering is necessary. And just in case you still aren't convinced that decluttering is for you, study these signs and look around your home for them. It's most certain that some of them exist around you. If you find them, then it's time to act. They include:

1. **You have lost track of the things you own**

From time to time, you stumble upon some stuff that you forget you even owned. They can be clothes that you don't even remember purchasing, books that you bought and never read, or even things that you can't even explain how they found their way into your house. The fact that you forget the presence of these things in your home simply goes to show that you really never needed them. No one ever forgets that one owns a car, because your car is important and is always in use. If you find things that fall into this category, then it's time to donate them to charity or do away with them through any other means.

2. It almost takes you forever to find stuff in your home

When clutter builds up, it's always hard to keep track of the valuables you own. How long do you spend looking for your underwear when it is time to dress up? What about your keys, is a torture finding them every morning? How about your smaller work tools like screwdrivers? Are they lying under the bed in the children's room? Your answers to these questions will specifically tell you how much you need to declutter your home.

In the absence of clutter, it's easier to find things within minutes or seconds. A decluttered home always has specific places for specific things because these things can be returned straight to their spaces after usage. On the other hand, clutter puts things out of place. It becomes traumatic to search for your stuff.

3. Colonization of work surfaces

It can either be the countertop in the kitchen, the dining table or the desk in your room, but whenever you begin to notice that clear surfaces in your home are beginning to lose their spaces then there's work to do. Clear surfaces are known to be some of the biggest collectors of clutter because there's much easier to dump things on them. They fill up quicker especially when you bring in a lot of things into your home. The most common of these work spaces include dresser tops, floor, countertops and tables.

4. Paper, books, magazines and more papers

Although we now live in a largely digitalized world, somehow papers find their way into our home. They come in the form of fliers, borrowed magazines, old books and pamphlets. For one reason or the other, you might find yourself lazy to deal with them and keep piling up until they cover up your desks and shelves. One question you may need to answer is when last you ever picked up any of those books to read. It might be time to turn them over to a local library or sell them proactively.

5. You feel overwhelmed in your own home

Clutter collects space in your home and alienates you. It'll make you feel unwelcomed even in your own house. As clutter builds up, you continue to find that the things you need to do are also building up. Soon you get frustrated because it seems virtually impossible to take care of all these tasks in one go. The thought of inviting friends over becomes a torture because you're not even proud of your own home. You know you need to do something about it but at this point the clutter have become so solidly grounded in your home that it seems like there's no way out.

6. You spend a lot of time cleaning the house

For people who own less stuff, it's much easier to clean up the house because the source of the disorganized can easily be identified. Cleaning a cluttered home is almost useless because the dirt will always find its way back into the house. Sometimes clutter is even responsible for harboring some of the dirt agents such as rodents or small insects.

Also, spending time organizing and reorganizing is a bad sign that you'll need to address. It simply means that you need to carry out a major reorganization in which you will assign permanent places for most of the stuff in the house.

BENEFITS OF DECLUTTERING

Finally, in this chapter it's necessary to consider some of the benefits of decluttering so that you can see the brighter picture and know why decluttering will be good for you and your home. The benefits of decluttering are wide ranging, encompassing facets of your life such as the mental, physical, health and even the emotional. Having a clean, decluttered, and well organized home is one of the major factors that can help you stay ahead of diseases and keep your psychology performing at its best. Here are some compelling reasons why you should considered decluttering:

1. It provides you with a freer schedule

As I stated before, the presence of clutter will always make you misplace things and not know where to find them when they are needed. When this clutter is dealt with, it instantly becomes easier to find things like your purse or keys whenever it is time to leave the house. If you have ever been late to a meeting because you were searching for your car keys, then you'll know what I'm suggesting. The time spent searching for your valuables can be spent doing other productive things if only you would decide to declutter and organize your home. Also, decluttering your home and leaving only the essentials helps you to reduce the constant need to organize and reorganize because now you can stay ahead and keep track of your belongings.

2. It provides you with some form of financial security

For you to succeed with your decluttering, you must realize a lot will have to change in your habits. Decluttering can only remain successful if these new habits are maintained. Once you have gotten rid of all of the things you no longer need, you can begin to place your focus on the valuable things around your life. When next you go out to make purchases from the mall, you'll notice how alert your mind will be to bring back only the necessities into your home.

3. You'll sleep better

The brain is more complicated than you know it, and sleep doesn't just come because you close your eyes. In reality, it's a more complex process than that. The brain is always involved in this decision making even while the eyes are closed. That's why you notice that you just wake up some nights with things bothering your mind, like wondering if you actually locked the front door before going to sleep. If you live in a cluttered space, then you'll find it daunting to get the best sleep. Your mind wants to see your home decluttered but your body isn't ready for that task so a conflict ensues that wards off sleep. The absence of clutter also helps in the sufficient flow of fresh air in your home, thus offering you better air to breathe while sleeping.

4. Better Concentration

A cluttered environment ultimately zaps you of your ability to concentrate. You'll likely keep bumping into things. As I have said before, your brain wants to see your surrounding decluttered because it works better in such as an environment. However, since your body is unwilling, you'll keep getting distracted because the brain will constantly remind you to deal with the clutter. Plus, clutter is a very frustrating thing to deal with, having to stay with stuffed cabinets and overloaded work desks. Decluttering your work spaces will make it easier for you to organize items and find them when needed.

5. Reduction of Anxiety

One of the major causes of anxiety is an overloaded life that has lost track of its essentials. This overload causes the brain to become over tasked and easily stressed. Your mind is left with the task of dealing with too many things. Your schedule becomes a wreck because there is too much to do and it is unorganized. You'll find that you'll feel stressed when a visitor is coming to your home for the first time. You're probably embarrassed because you wonder how he or she perceives you after coming into your home and seeing how you live. Once clutter is dealt with, you'll notice the kind of freedom that will become evident in your life. No more embarrassing moments or stressful thoughts about visitors will occur.

6. Increased productivity and creativity

Some people say that as long as your workspace in the office is clean and organized, you can manage clutter at home. But remember that most times solutions to some office problems come to us while we're at home. If the brain is constantly in a battle against clutter, there's no way it can able to perform and produce the best results. Also, a decluttered environment helps to improve mood and eliminate depression, thereby providing you with enough mental energy for brainstorming.

CHAPTER TWO: THE MINDSET FOR DECLUTTERING

For you to have continuous success with your decluttering endeavor, there has to be a major change of mindset. It's only natural that you fall into the category of people who love to acquire new things, who love to bask in the thrill of a brand new purchase. It's normal in the average human being. Take some time and probe your mind and find out how long the pleasures of new purchases last. Chances are that they don't last more than a few months then they disappear into thin air. At one point all of your attention is fixed on buying one trendy outfit or gadget; and once you get it, you become bored and begin to chase other things. It's typical because the human pursuit of a purpose gives our lives meaning, but there are more relevant things that we can focus on with our minds. Thus, this logic is the essence of decluttering.

When starting up decluttering, you'll need to make a conscious effort to look beyond the ordinary and see beyond materialism. This is the foundation of decluttering. If this point is missed, then there's little or no hope of success. Take your mind away from owning more possessions to gaining experiences and meeting people. Invest in things that matter. It'll take some time for you to get comfortable, but the ultimate reward will be worth it. You might also find it quiet hard to select items you no longer need, items you should do away with, but with time you will begin to identify them. With this newly adopted mindset, you'll then notice that the urge to bring in more things into your home will be reduced. This is where your success as a minimalist begins to manifest itself. Soon you'll begin to reap the benefits of decluttering such as more time on your hand, money and energy saved.

DAILY HABITS TO DEVELOP TO HELP YOU WITH YOUR DECLUTTERING

These rituals listed here are daily habits you'll need to adopt for a continuously decluttered life. They'll certainly take some time to be developed, so you'll need some form of consistency to see success:

1. **Become a gatekeeper for your home**

You have to literally become a gatekeeper to protect your home from the invasion of junks and clutter. Find out what comes in and what goes out of your home. Are your children bringing in unnecessary junks into the house without your knowledge? This can include toys of other kids in the neighborhood or just some other play things. Being a gatekeeper means that you have to correct them and show them why they should stop. You also have to be a gatekeeper for your own self. Sometimes you may bring in clutter into your home without knowing what you have done so. This gatekeeper consciousness will help to keep you in check and prevent such excesses.

2. One comes in, one has to go

Clutter is basically born out of accumulation. You have fifteen pair of jeans trousers, but you saw one so irresistible in the mall today, so you want to get it. You can get it, but you now realize that one of your other pairs of jeans at home must leave the house either to be donated or given to a friend. This principle also applies to broken and spoiled items in your home. You own a malfunctioning television and you finally come across some money to get a new one, so there's no need keeping the old when you can sell off its parts to a repairer. Don't fall for the temptation of taking the old equipment and clothing to the basement. You're basically just transferring clutter from one part of the house to another. You've solved nothing.

3. Keep your surfaces clean

As I noted earlier, clean and clear surfaces are some of the biggest magnets of clutter. You work into a room with a pile of clothes and the best place to keep them is the neat laid bed. All you want to do is get rid of the load on your hands and drop them somewhere. You go into the kitchen with dishes and drop them on the sink and zoom out to the sitting room to catch the latest series on your favorite TV show. That habit of dump and pile has to stop. Each day, go around your home and ensure that all of the surfaces that should be cleared are actually clutter free. Take books off the desks and put them in the shelf. Wash the dishes and put them in the cabinet. If you buy new dishes, get rid of some of the old ones in a yard sale or something like that. Make sure that you spend each morning ensuring that all surfaces in your home remain cleared.

4. Try to involve your family or roommates

Decluttering can get quite frustrating especially when the people you share your home with aren't helping you out. If you're able to buy them into the vision the process will be a whole lot easier for you with everyone carrying out their own portions of the tasks. It's definitely going to be harder getting your lodge mates to comply but you can still try. With children it is quite easy because they're still in their formative years and you have some level of authority over them. Make your children get rid of their shoes, their toys and their clothes once they come into the house. At the initial stage of the training, it might take a lot of hard work to convince your kids of the benefits of decluttering, but with time you'll notice that they key in naturally.

5. Take 10 minutes each day to search for clutter in the house

At the beginning of your decluttering process, clutter will remain persistent. At this point you'll still be at the developing level of decluttering skills. There are no worries, though. What you should do is to ensure that you spend at least 10 minutes every day going through your home to identify clutter that may have accumulated since the day before. This way you cut off the clutter at the beginning of its growth; plus, it'll help you to identify the major places to watch for the development of clutter. For some other homes 10 minutes won't be enough to get rid of clutter every day, especially when the home is a large one. You can take more time to get the job done.

6. Tidy up once you're done

The basic point here is to allow clutter not to build up. Do everything in your power to avoid this build up. Once you're done reading a book or magazine, send it to the shelf. Don't dump the plates in the sink for days at a time. Wash them after every meal and stack them back into the dish rack. Never let your clutter alert go cold for any reason at all.

This same principle should apply to the kids. Make them return their toys to appropriate points in their rooms once they are through playing with them. Your work tools shouldn't be left lying at different spots where you last worked. Send them back into the toolbox once you're done using them. But before you can begin to practice this habit, you must first have a place for everything in your house.

7. Handle all paperwork such as physical mail, bills, or receipts once they arrive

Papers are one of the most common causes of junks. They grow so slowly that you never notice it until they colonize your home and almost chase you out of it. Settle the mail once it arrives. Don't leave it for a later time. If you're too busy to deal with your mail immediately, you should have basket where you'll put in mail that should be handled later. Don't allow this basket to get too full. Have a specific time per week when you will sort through them. If possible, buy and place a paper shredder close to the basket where you can toss in some of the settled mails with personal information so that they can be discarded properly.

LEARNING GRATITUDE AND MINDFULNESS FOR MINIMALISM

Mindfulness and minimalism are two concepts that are constantly paired together because of how important they are to the achievement of one or the other. Mindfulness can be described as intentional living, living with a purpose, and a reason. Mindfulness also helps you to keep your focus on the valuable and important things in your life so you can live with gratitude. Here are some ways in which mindfulness and gratitude can help you with your decluttering:

1. Enjoying the present

Mindfulness helps you as an individual to live in and enjoy the present. Most people live in the regret of their pasts or in the anxiety for their future. These two factors are some of the reasons why most of us never amount to anything in the present. Your vision is divided and the next outcome is that you stumble and fall. Mindfulness and minimalism will teach you how to be grateful for the now while preparing for a better future with lots of light in it.

One way to begin to let go of the past is to release things you own that remind you about that point in your life, things that bring back those memories. Keep only the things that are of utmost importance, things that bring new love into your life. The future clutter refers to that clutter that forms as a result of things we keep in case we need them in the future. Of course, it's sensible to keep stuff for the future, but there should be a limit. You don't start storing baby things while still a college students. It's viable to store but that isn't the right time and soon clutter will form.

2. Free yourself of sentimental attachments

There's one key piece of advice you should take from here: you should begin to see the things you own for what they are. They're simply things and nothing more. Once you begin to attach more to them, a problem begins to form. Starting up the decluttering process will help to remove any form of attachments you may have with some of your possessions such that they almost begin to control you.

The mindfulness that comes with minimalism is one that makes us probe the reason why we own some stuff, to understand the reason for their existence in our lives. This way everything that comes into our home becomes a thing that can only add value in the long run. Taking away anything that has failed the test of value is only creating space for more important things.

3. Appreciate the journey

Minimalism is basically about the process, the journey towards perfection. There's no end line where you reach and then say, "I'm done." In fact, minimalism is an everyday journey that needs to be enjoyed for you to remain consistent. It's a lesson where you learn contentment, to appreciate your space and how to make big and meaningful changes in your live over a long period of time. All in all, you'll learn patience while practicing decluttering.

BEFORE YOU MAKE ANOTHER PURCHASE, ASK YOURSELF THESE VITAL QUESTIONS

As stated, minimalism is always in a constant battle with materialism. You'll have to fuel your minimalist instincts so that it comes on top and subdues materialism. For long time minimalists, it'll be quite easier to overcome the urge to buy and consume, but for some readers of this book who might just be getting exposed to the concept of decluttering the possibility of going back to the vomit is very high. Remember what we went through about being a gatekeeper? The contents of this subtopic will provide you with questions to help control this urge to re-stuff clutter into your home:

1. **Do I really need this or am I tempted to buy it just because I can see it on sale?**

If there's one tip to watch out for throughout your decluttering journey, it's an impulse purchase. Impulse purchase simply means buying without the extra thought, buying simply because you want to buy. Most of the items you end up buying during an impulse purchase always end up as junk or clutter, because their true values were never tested before purchase was made.

The best thing to do once you come across an item on sale which you feel you may need isn't to buy it. Ignore that item for that day and give it sometime. If the need keeps reoccurring and bothering you, then you know it is a genuine need and it is time to get the item. Sometimes, after that first impulse to buy the item, you'll later notice how you totally forgot about it, how unimportant it had always been. This isn't to say that you shouldn't reward yourself occasionally, but ensure that there's always a limit so that your need for pleasure does not override your decluttering instincts. Remember that our main aim here is to live life as intentionally as possible.

2. **What if I can borrow or rent this?**

Before you decide to make a purchase, it's important that you go through your stuff and check if you don't already own something that can serve the purpose of the other item you want to buy. Sometimes, items we have at home can be repurposed to serve other purposes, if only we decide to be more creative. So try to dig deeper.

The same also go for items that can be borrowed or rented. Let's say there's a tool you make use of once in six months and for the rest of the year it just lies dormant in the basement. It's better that you rent that tool whenever you need it than to spend money on it and have its value deteriorate over a period of time if left unused. If possible, you can borrow from a neighbor. The job might probably last a few hours and they won't mind. Another option is to call a professional service to get the job done for a pay. All of these will help save you the stress of buying something that will eventually lead to clutter.

3. **Am I buying this because of external influence?**

Trends are exciting, but remember that they fade. It's very easy to hop into the bandwagon, but the regrets might soon follow suit. This isn't to say that you should begin to dress like a hipster or adopt an unfashionable life, but know where to draw the line. Don't allow yourself be propelled to make a purchase simply because someone you know has made that purchase and is cajoling you to do the same. That can be a disastrous decision that can undermine your decluttering struggles.

4. Are the quality and value of the product worth it?

Your major aim as a decluttering agent is to improve the quality of life both for yourself and for the people around you. The way to do that is to begin to improve the quality and value of the items you purchase. It's better to own 10 shirts of the best quality and material than to own 50 that are worn out, ugly and of low quality. The joy of spending your money to purchase things of quality is something that will last you a long time. You'll learn contentment from it.

5. Can my financial capacity at the moment manage this purchase?

This is the most critical question you'll need to ask yourself. Making purchases when your finances are struggling is a dangerous thing to do. You'll run into debts and debt itself is some form of clutter because it chokes life out of you. No matter the quality and value of the product, if you presently don't have the money to make a purchase, then ignore it for now. Whenever you're stable, you can come back and get it.

CHAPTER THREE: THE BASICS OF DECLUTTERING

Before we begin to explore and understand the process of decluttering different aspects of the home, it's necessary that we first understand the basis of decluttering, the techniques that will assist you. In this chapter, I'll teach you some of the most common methods required in taking care of the clutter in different part of the homes. It might take you a while to master them, but when you finally do, the job will become a lot easier to perform.

1. **Knowing where to start**

For people who are decluttering for the first time, the major drawback is always the question of knowing where to start. When you go through your belongings and notice the presence of clutter, it's easy to feel overwhelmed and believe that you cannot do it. I advise you not to subscribe to such thoughts. They only last for a while until you decide to take action.

The first thing to do is to pick up a room. It can either be the kitchen or the storeroom or the basement. That choice is left to your discretion. Once you select a room, the next thing is to identify its greatest point of clutter assemblage. Are the drawers overstuffed with clothes? Are there moving boxes lying in hidden corners and filled with useless items? If yes, clear them out punctually. Find a small space in the room and remove everything in those drawers and boxes. You'll need to create a small open space where you will be able to dump some of these items.

This will help to provide you with a perspective of starting afresh, which is necessary for your decluttering journey.

2. **Categorization**

Once you've purged the clutter from their hiding places, it's better sort them out into categories. There are three major categories that items in your clutter can fall into: The items to be kept, those to be discarded and those to be donated. You can make use of marked boxes to place items that have been sorted out so as to prevent them from mixing together.

You have to be sincere with yourself if you really want to see any success with your decluttering. Push your sentiments aside and soften your attachments to possessions. You'll come across items that will be hard to let go of while decluttering. Don't worry about them. Create a special category for items like these that you'll come back to on a later date.

Now, the discard category will be made up of items that are basically worthless in every sense of the word. These are items that may have outlived their shelf life and can no longer be repurposed or reused for other things. This is why I first warned you to drop sentimentality, because it'll hinder you from discarding the things you are to discard due to your perceived attachment to them. If you want to be more creative, you can consider recycling items in this category so that you don't litter the environment with non-biodegradable junks.

The keep box, as the name implies, refers to those items you may want to keep, items that still have some value. Don't go about tossing items into the keep box just because your mind tells you that you have to keep them. You must make a conscious effort to ensure that each item that makes it back into the keep box has value. For an item to make it into the keep box, it's vital that you can pick at least three ways of which it is still important and cannot be replaced. Any item that fails this test should be thrown into the donation box.

Finally, the donation box is the box that contains things of value that you no longer need. At this point you'll have to be truthful to yourself. You'll come across items in your home that are useful but haven't been used in a longer time. It would be better to give them out to people who need them instead of hoarding them. Or don't you think so? These items include clothes you have outgrown but still love; toys lying in the basement even though your kids have all left high school, and books that you no longer need. It might seem hard letting go of these things, but in the end you'll reap the benefits of a freer home.

3. A place for each item

A major core principle in minimalism and decluttering is having a space or home for everything that stays in your home. Each item that you own should have a space where it'll feel most comfortable, a place where they can be easily found and returned to when their job is done. Without this, every other thing you do in decluttering is simply a waste of precious time.

Now that you've successfully sorted out the clutter in your home, it's time for you to map out designated spaces for each of the items that you want to keep. The basis of creating space should depend on how much you use the object, how fragile it is and how near you'll want the item to be when needed. Luckily, some parts of the house already come with some of the rooms broken down into compartments to help you out with your storage. The kitchen comes with cabinets, the storeroom with shelves and the bedrooms with wardrobes. These can help you out while sorting out places where you can categorize and store these items.

Note that it's one goal to create spaces for these items in your home and it's another thing to be disciplined enough not to leave your arrangement plan. You'll have to get your household as involved as possible so that you don't end up getting frustrated. To ensure the success of this arrangement, you'll need to exercise more discipline by returning clothes to the hanger once you pull them off and taking magazines back to the shelf after reading.

Take a few minutes of each day to return items back to their spaces in the home. This will help you identify some major spots where clutter forms and accumulates itself.

4. Keep surfaces cleared

When decluttering your home, you'll come across various surfaces in different parts of the house. I've already explained how clutter forms on surfaces, because they are clutter magnets. Remember that your surfaces should not be used as a storage point in the house. If there's ever going to be a need for that, then the items to be kept on that surface must be well arranged. These procedures will help you out in cleaning up a decluttered surface whenever you come across them.

I. Take out every single thing on that surface, both those that belong there and those that don't. After decluttering, the items that should be there will find their way there so don't worry about that for now.

II. Stand back from the empty surface and try to evaluate its purpose in your home. What exactly do you want to use this surface for? There's a possibility that you'll want to use for another purpose entirely so it's your decision that will ultimately influence the items that will find their way back to that surface.

III. The next step will be to select the items that should sit on that surface. To ensure that you have success with your surface cleaning, I advise that not more than five objects should be found on each surface. Just select five of the items and find another home for the other items. The surface remains as cleared as possible. You can add one or two items just to beautify the surface, but don't allow it to become too jam-packed.

IV. Finally, it's not only about clearing up surfaces. If extra care isn't taken, your surfaces can become cluttered even before the day is over. Extra measures will have to be taken to ensure the constant declutter of those surfaces. For example, you'll have to discipline yourself not to dump items on surfaces simply because there is nowhere else to dump them. This also refers to the floor.

Never drop anything on the floor especially when there is already a designated space for that item. Another measure to take in protecting your surfaces is to ensure that you wipe and clean them at least thrice every week. As you wipe, be meticulous to take away any item that shouldn't be found on that surface. Discard those that need to be removed, so that the surfaces can return back to its decluttered state.

Another factor that leads to the accumulation of clutter is procrastination. There will always be something that will want to make you leave your surfaces to be cleaned up later. You'll hear your mind say to you, "Just dump it there for a few minutes. You can come back to it later and clear it up." Please don't succumb to such a voice. Every clutter should be dealt with immediately they are brought into the house. If you bring in clothes from the laundry line, they should be folded and packed into the wardrobe and not left on the bed for later. This negligence is one way in which clutter begins to form without your detection.

5. Levels of Organization

In decluttering and arrangement, levels of organization refer to a process of organizing items in your home in such a way that the ones that serve the same purpose are group together so that they can be easily found when needed. For example, this will help you not to find the scissors lying among your cosmetics in your room, or the screwdriver mixed with spoons on the kitchen shelf. It just makes life a lot easier when you have these things already group up in your home. All you will need to do in go to that point in the house where they've been grouped together and select the things you'll need and return them back once you're done.

One benefit of going along with this form of classification is that it helps you to keep stock of the things you own. To illustrate, if you're going to get extra supplies, it's easy to look into our crotchet tool box and count the number of wool balls you have and how many more will be needed. The case would have been totally different if they were all scattered around the house. You'll soon discover that you never needed to buy some items in the home since they were already there in the first place, hiding at different corners.

These organizational levels will also help you out in cutting off the excesses in your home. While making these groupings, you'll be able to identify those things you have an excess of and know how to deal with them. Go through each of the categories and as yourself questions. Do you really need five pairs of scissors? How about more than a hundred ceramic mugs? Some of those things constitute clutter and the best time to get rid of them is now.

Once you have been able to group these items into their various categories such as cutleries, tailoring equipment, toys, etc., it'll be time to find the perfect spots for them in the home. Obviously, you'll have to keep them at the points in the home where they will be most needed. You don't carry your box of tools to the kitchen and take the cutlery to the workshop. No. For some other classes, you'll need to creatively brainstorm and find the perfect places to keep them. And once you have found the perfect spaces and stored them in this spaces, you'll have to ensure that the objects found in those categories are always returned to their homes and never left lying around in other parts of the home.

6. Set a limit

At this point, all the items in your home should have been effectively classified so that you've no problem finding them and returning them back to their spaces. But there is another issue that we will have to handle, which the problem of not knowing when enough is enough. For some people, buying and purchasing more and more items into their homes is the only way they can be assured that they'll never go stranded or need anything again. This is a flawed school of thought. In fact, the reverse is the case. You're able to stay more organized when you are able to manage the little you own. This is where the importance of categorization comes in. When things are categorized, it's easier to keep stock and know when to stop buying one items into one category.

One funny example I always love to refer to are socks. Those are easy to misplace in the house; and because of this, owners are prone to keep buying and buying more of them until the whole house is filled with them. For someone who has managed to stay ahead and organize them into pairs, not only will it be easy to find them, but it'll help you know when you have enough of them. When they're inventories in this way, items from one category don't end up overflowing their spaces into other spaces. This way clutter is controlled.

Setting these limits will not only help you but your family member who will benefit immensely from it. Teaching them the benefits of setting limits and preventing and overflow will certainly make the job easier for you in the long run. Not only should items be classified into their various categories, but people living together in a home should also be given personal spaces which they shouldn't cross. This arrangement will help teach boundaries and organization to people your home and help them to appreciate small spaces of existence.

7. Work with a routine

Never forget that decluttering is an ongoing process for as long as you live. Once you relax and lose your guard, clutter will match back into your home and re-conquer its space. This is why you need to be on guard, to be watchful and observant, so this weed doesn't find a space to grow up again. I've listed out some key habits that will help you out in dealing with clutter, habits that you'll need to take seriously if you want to achieve any success. The difference between one person that begins to declutter and continues to live a declutter life and another who just gets frustrated and stops along the way is habits. Habits define who we are and what goes on in our lives.

To build up these habits, you'll need to develop routines that will work for you. You must understand yourself best and you know what works and what doesn't. Incorporate this knowledge into building up a character that will challenge the build-up of clutter in your home. One vital part of this routine is the control of materialism. Find out those things that cause to you go and get impulse shopping. Sometimes it can be friends, so you might need to let them know why you may not be going out with them the next time they're going shopping. For others, it can be mailing subscriptions and browser ads. The best tip is canceling some of these subscriptions and/or block the ads so that you don't get tempted.

Finally, you'll need to set goals and achieve them. Plus, there should be rewards for you whenever you reach your goals. If you own a journal or a diary, write down all of the things you'll want to achieve with your decluttering, all the habits you'll want to imbibe before a certain period of time is over. From time to time, you can tick them off as you achieve them. This will afford some form of encouragement to keep you going. You can also reward yourself when you hit your goals. Take pictures of each decluttered space and savor them occasionally, so you're reminded of the beauty inherent of a decluttered environment.

CHAPTER FOUR: DEALING WITH KITCHEN

As I stated earlier, you can start your decluttering process from any part of your home that you deem fit, but for the sake of this book, we'll consider the kitchen first.

As a result said, I can't begin to explain the importance of having a clean and clear kitchen devoid of clutter. People used to say jokingly that the kitchen is the mitochondria of the home, powerhouse where energy flows from. If the kitchen gets infected, the home will suffer. And the truth is that a person's kitchen tells a lot about one's personality. A tidy kitchen means an organized individual, someone I'd like to be friends with personally. A cluttered kitchen simply shows an unorganized and untidy person. So you have to get you kitchen in order so that you home begins to take a decluttered shape and path.

WHERE TO BEGIN IN THE KITCHEN

The first thing to do is to look around your kitchen and try to identify key areas in which clutter have formed. The identification of these zones will make the work a lot easier for you. Some examples of things you should look for are:

- Is the kitchen counter littered with school books, mails or other items that should not be found there?
- How disorganized are the drawers that hold the kitchen utensils?
- Is your kitchen equipment carefully organized so that it's easier to find them?
- How compliant are family members about returning items back to their spaces after usage?

These are some of the assessments you'll have to make to begin the decluttering process. For your kitchen, there may be more considerations such as the need to add more shelf spaces and all, but these are the major areas.

Once you have been able to identify these clutter zones, then you can take all of the clutter out and pile them on the floor of the kitchen. Classify them into items that you'll keep, those that will be discarded, and those that will be donated. Remember that you must be truthful to yourself to ever achieve any success. You'll come across utensils you may not have used in a longer time but will want to keep. Ask yourself what you are doing with three blenders when you only use one? Look around for the excesses in the kitchen and the spaces they have occupied. These are the place you'll have to work on and hone.

While in the kitchen, don't forget the store area. There are probably some empty cans, sachets and box that have been left lying around and occupying space simply because you have been too lazy to take them to the trash. Most of the sensitive cooking ingredients like sugar that attract insects should be stored in air tight containers so that are protected from air and moisture. Take out the cans and bottles in the refrigerator. Then using a damp cloth, clean up the compartments that collect water. Chances are, you'll come across canned foods that have expired.

These tips will help you in dealing with your lower kitchen cabinets:
- Line your cabinets with some material, either paper or vinyl, to further add some aesthetic value to the cabinet.
- Leave enough space in the lower cabinets where you can store up heavy kitchen equipment where they can be easily fished out for usage.
- You should watch out for the accumulation of plastic containers for take-outs. When their lids get lost, they almost become useless, so there's no need in keeping them.
- If you don't have a rack for your pots and stoves, it's best to stack them in order of size when putting them into the cabinet. That is, the largest remains close to the ground, with the second largest inside of it, then the next largest until you get to the smallest.

For upper cabinets, the case should be entirely different. They should hold more of the breakable items where they will far from the children's reach. You'll have to a little bit more careful when trying to clear up that space since you will be climbing on a stool or a chair to elevate yourself. Take out some time to review the objects in the cabinets and find select those that you will want to store and those that you will be giving away. Then you categorize the items in each cabinet so the items in the cabinets can be easily sorted out when needed. These tips will help you out when arranging items in the upper cabinets:
- Only items that are used on daily basis should be kept in the upper cabinets. For example, keeping heavy chinaware that is used only during the holidays will end up weighing down and destroying the upper cabinets, so it's best they're stored securely out of sight in a lower cabinet.
- Everyday dishes are best stored in a rack close to the sink for easy loading after each wash.
- If you come across any chipped glassware, mugs or plates, it's vital that you toss them out. They're highly susceptible to the breakage during any slight heating or accident.

KITCHEN APPLIANCES AND GADGETS
Most kitchen appliances and gadgets are quite expensive and this makes it harder to let go of them. But the truth is that some of them still have to be discarded because they've

likely lived past their potential and are simply taking up space in your home. Some appliances have been stacked up over the years and now you have more than one of such appliances. Select those you hardly use and donate them. If you come across those that you no longer use because of damage, then this is the best time to work on it for repair. Remember that the goal here is to only store items that will be of great value in your home.

How many of such kitchen items do you need lying on the counter and occupying precious space? The answer is only a few of the most necessary ones. Some appliances on your counter might still be valuable but are not used every day. These one should be tucked away and keep in a space in the lower cabinet to be brought back only on days when they will be used. If you lack space in your kitchen to keep these appliances that aren't used regularly, you can take some of them into a secure part of the basement or attic.

Beneath the sink
Most people like to ignore this space in their kitchen, but you shouldn't. Cleaning up this part of the kitchen might take you a while. Open up the small, dark cabinet underneath the sink, and see what lies there. Perhaps there is a broken pipe, roaches lying around or a small, stagnant pool formed over the week? Call for repairs if you come across such a breakage and clean up any water that may have accumulated there. Add or replace waterproof materials that line the cabinet.

Sponges should be well placed so that water dripping from them after usage does not destroy any sensitive material. Place them in a drained container close to the sin where so that any water dripping from them goes directly into the sink. You can also install metal hooks on the side of a cabinet where brushes, gloves, and sponges can be hung.

If you keep cleaners, detergents, soaps or pesticides under the sink, ensure not to put any edible stuff alongside them in that space to prevent contamination and subsequent food poisoning.

Spices, condiments, herbs and seasonings
Most store up condiments, seasonings and herbs in glass jars that are kept in a separate cabinet for easy reach. That cabinet will need to be cleaned up, too. Take your time and remove all the jars in the cabinets. Put them all into a large box and clean the cabinet, removing cobwebs and accumulated dust. Before you put back the jars into the cabinet, go through them and find out those that need to be tossed out because of cracks or any other defects. Others may not have held any new seasoning in months. Be vigilant to fill

up again or take out the glass jar from the kitchen to conserve space. For such items that come with an expiration date, be careful to check that they haven't exceeded this date.

The best place to store up your spices and herbs in a drawer under the stove so that it's easier to reach for them while cooking. Another brilliant option that helps you save space is to make use of a magnetic rack on the wall nearest to your stove where you can easily reach out and grab the spices. If there are spices that you use infrequently, then you should buy smaller jars of such so that they don't go to waste.

Cooking Utensils
Utensils are generally always located close to the cooking area where they can be reached. You can place them on a countertop to dry after washing with their lids in place. If your pots are kept in a stack in a cabinet, there are racks that can help you keep your lids organized. Of all of these, the best option is the availability of a pots rack on the wall where pots can be hung with their handles on the wall.

There are small cooking items that you use more frequently than other such as whisk, grater and wooden spoons. You can set all of these in a ceramic pitcher close to the stove, so they can remain closer to you.

Baking items should be stored in various compartments depending majorly on the frequency of use. Some families make more pastries than others, so it depends. But baking items should be closer to the oven. You might also want to have a baking drawer close to the oven where you can keep items such as measuring cups and spoons and others that you make use of more often.

The Drawers
The kitchen drawers are among some of the most important spaces in the whole house. They hold important items that we make use of everyday, items that should be protected from dirt or contamination. These include utensils, foils, spices or flatware. Because of this, it's necessary that this space remains as clean and organized as possible so that cooking items can be picked at ease and also kept clean.

First, open up each of the drawers and make a small assessment of the items that are currently present in them. Also take note of how disorganized the space has become. You point of action will be to categorize and find items that may have missed their places and are in the wrong drawers. Empty each of the drawers and place their contents on the countertop. Remember that this is only a process that will last one minutes, so be quick and take off those items from the countertop and return it to their decluttered shape.

Clean up each of those drawers and get rid of cobwebs or dust that may have clogged the spaces. You can spray some pesticides and close it up to kill insects damaging the wood. But be careful when doing that, especially when the drawer holds sensitive items.

Once the drawer is clean, take your time to sort through the items before placing them into the drawer. Are there utensils that have been in there for too long without usage? There's no use keeping those ones that come with cracks. They serve no purpose. It's best to discard them. Select those that should be giving away and stack them into the donation box so that it is easy to move them around without causing more damage. If you come across items that no longer belong in one drawer, punctually move them to the drawer where you feel they'll be more useful. If you come across duplicates e.g four whisks, three colanders etc., be proactive to get rid of some of them. At least have two of each just in case of a necessity. Also keep your eyes open for expired or spoiled herbs.

The Refrigerator
Whenever I think about refrigerators, I think: space alert! Refrigerators or deep freezers are always quite large and they end up take up large chunks of space. Sometimes they can get faulty and there might be a need to get a newer one, but don't discard the older. One solution here might be to place one of them in the garage, kitchen storeroom, or any other free room in the house that has enough space to accommodate. Also, take note to give extra care to your refrigerators. They have a way of subtly accumulating clutter over a period of time. I used to humorously think that the only difference between a refrigerator and a waste bin is that one cools. The refrigerator has now become so abused as a dumping ground for leftovers and others until we forget about them, and they become spoiled.

To start up the decluttering process, take everything out of the fridge and clean the inner spaces. Get rid of all the stain marks and water. Then categorize the items that belong in the refrigerator. These can include categories such as diary, fresh products, fruits, vegetables, and condiments. The classification will basically depend on your discretion since you're most familiar with the contents of your refrigerator.

The Countertops
The beauty of clear and clean countertops cannot be overemphasized enough in your kitchen. They're a blessing and also assist you to get work done as quickly as possible. Items will always find their way to your kitchen countertop, but it's best that you allow them to be as clutter free as possible. One quick way to achieve this clutter free zone is by putting away everything from the countertops once you're through with them. Declutter the countertop after each cooking or after each meal, because this is the time in which they accumulate the most clutter.

To start up the decluttering process, start by removing appliances that you don't make use of everyday. They'll be easy to identify. They'll include those items that you use occasionally, equipment that are always coated in dust until the day you decide to dust them off and make use of them. Appliances like these should be your major target. Depending on how frequently these items are used, you can now know where to place them. For example, appliances that you make use of once in a month can be kept in the cabinet under the countertop. Other appliances that may be used only once in three months can be taken to the garage and arranged to conserve space. If you have some more space in your kitchen cabinets, you can send some of the everyday appliances into those cabinets to produce extra space on the countertop.

The next step in clearing the countertop is dealing with other miscellaneous objects lying on them. There's a high chance that some items lying on the countertops can be kept in other spaces apart from the countertop. Go through the items lying there and ask yourself if they really need to be on that counter top. If you have correctly categorized the items in your kitchen, it'll be quite easy for you to find a different home for the items lying on the countertop. Most of those items lying in that space are basically there because you haven't given them a home. Once you settle that, they'll never find their way to the countertop and constitute clutter. The major goal here should be to leave as little as possible on the counter top.

The suggestions will assist you in producing the best from your countertop decluttering:
- Keys are some of the major constituents of clutter on a countertop and the best way to deal with them by getting a key rack or bowl on the countertop where keys can be placed once they're brought into the house.
- Cookbooks should remain on the main bookshelf in the house and never on the countertop in the kitchen. In fact, having your cookbooks constantly lying on the countertops is one way to help them get dog-eared and wet faster. Only visit your cookbooks on the shelf when you need to and take down any recipe you may want to experiment with as needed.
- You can keep drying racks on the sinks instead of putting them on the countertops. This is necessary for many reasons such as preventing the countertop from accumulating water from drained dishes and also providing proximity to the sink while washing plates.
- Finally, the countertops should be cleared up every night after dishes have been washed and arranged. Always make sure that you wake up each morning with a clean and clear countertop.

CHAPTER FIVE: THE MASTER BEDROOM

Loving or hating your master bedroom all depends on the efforts you put into shaping it into the perfect sanctuary. The decluttering of your master bedroom might require you to sacrifice a few days to it. This is one of the most important spaces in your home, a place where you spend most of your time. It should be as spacious, calm, and organized as possible for you to enjoy every single moment spent living in it. One of the major benefits of a decluttered home, as we discussed earlier, is the presence of better sleep. This is where that benefit comes into play. A decluttered bedroom will always provide you with peace of mind, better air flow, and increased sleep in the long run.

A conscious effort will need to be made to reclaim this space. You'll have to take a set of determined and well directed actions to see the success you require from decluttering your master bedroom. Some of the simpler actions and habit change that will be necessary include:

- Clearing and making the bed every morning. As simple as this sounds, it can make a great change in the ways in which your room is organized. The next time you wake up and lay your bed, stand back and observe the peace you feel looking as the clear surface. The best way to describe it is: Peaceful. I bet that this is a sight you'll want to wake up to every time you walk into the room.
- The next place to consider is under the bed. This is a sensitive zone and if care is not taken, a lot can pile up there and affect your health and sleep. Dust, bedbugs, and rodents are some of the most common examples of this.
- Drawer tops, tables and desks should also be handled to get rid of the most common clutter constituents.

Here are some of the major signs in a bedroom that shows you need to declutter as soon as possible:

- The bed is always unarranged, with ruffled blankets and foreign objects lying on it.
- Clothes never find their way into the overstuffed closets since there's never enough space for them.
- The surfaces in the room are always jam-packed with items without homes because the spaces in the room have been designated for the storage of different categories of objects.
- You always find it hard to find things like keys and undergarments whenever needed.

STARTING UP

The most important step to take towards decluttering the bedroom is to look around and identify objects that shouldn't there. Find those that should be in a different part of the home. Some of these will include the coffee mug lying on the bedside table or completed books that should be in the library. Pick each of these and return them to their right spots in your home. Also take note of items that have become excessive in your home. Are the picture frames hanging the wall making the place look disorganized? What about the decorative objects, the pillows, and stuffed animals on the bed? Have they become too much?

Take out time and take out the things. Select those that should be trashed and those that should be kept. If you spend more of your time working in your bedroom, then you'll have to make an effort to tidy the room of stacks of papers and other materials. Distinguish your work space from your relaxation space, so that the two don't mix and end up frustrating you.

Under the bed

Look under the bed and assess any junk residing there. What can you identify? How long have those items been there? Should they be there? If yes, then how long? If no, then where do they need to be? Bring out everything under the bed: then make a selection of the items that will remain there, those that will be taken away to other spaces and those that will be discarded. I urge you to get rid of everything lying under the bed, but I also know that it can be a useful space for the storage of frequently used items. This is also why it should be protected from dust and bugs invasion.

You'll need to take special note of the following if you want to successfully make use of under the bed as a storage space:

- That space should never be a place for hiding stuff you're ashamed of. Instead of using it to store dirty clothes, send them over to the laundry where they belong.
- If you store clothes in that space, then ensure that whatever container you use is neat and well-covered. Never keep damp clothes in that space.
- Get a bed shirt that you can use to cover up the space so that the items lying there don't remain exposed.

The Nightstands

Nightstands are to be used to harbor items that will be needed at night during an emergency. Unfortunately, due to the presence of clutter they can become something else. It shouldn't be so. Everything on your nightstand should be there intentionally. Nightstands should never be a pick and dump space for placing anything that has no place.

The main question here should be: What should be on your nightstand? What are the items that you make use of at most night? Make a short list of not more than seven items that should be on your nightstand. Surfaces like the nightstand are very prone and receptive to the accumulation of clutter so you'll have to stick to the list you make.

If your nightstand comes with a drawer underneath it, then you can maximize this space to store excess items. Also, make a note to return items back to the spaces once you're through with them.

THE BEDROOM SURFACES

When you're done dealing with the general clutter in the house, the next place to face will be the clutter resident on the bedroom surfaces. Scan through the room and identify the places where clutter is most evident and work on them one after another. Remove everything on the surface and reevaluate the use of that surface. What are the things that will be returning there and why? Find out places that the other stray items should be kept and take them there.

Clutter always forms on the dresser due to the over population of cosmetics and other accessories. Some of these can be sent into the drawers underneath the surface where they'll be brought out only when necessary. Pick the most important accessories needed on the table top and send the rest to other spaces in the room.

A small bowl can be placed on the dresser to hold buttons, needles, threads and wool balls. Placing them in a bowl will help the dresser stay more organized and prevent them from falling off and rolling under the table.

If you love to spend the night with books, then it's advisable that you get a small book shelf for the bedside so that your night books stay as organized as possible. There are many options available to you, such as purchasing a secondhand bookshelf or buying smaller ones from Amazon.

THE DRAWERS

The most problematic drawers are usually those filled with undergarments and other smaller clothing materials. In decluttering the drawers in the master bedroom, it's necessary that you talk to anybody you may be sharing the space with you. Ask him or her for permission to go ahead with the cleaning or seek one's participation in the process.

As always, you'll need to take out everything in each drawer to start up the decluttering process. Don't forget to be on the alert and keep your eyes open for items that should not be have been there in the first place. Clean the inside of each drawer and put in some camphor of air fresher, to help repel insects and rodents. Begin to sort through all the items heaped from each drawer and categorize them into items to be kept, those to be discarded and those to be given out. Also keep your eye open for items that need to be washed. Don't toss them under the bed. Instead, take them straight to the laundry until you're ready to wash them.

The basic example of items that shouldn't find their way back into the drawers are those that are tattered, permanently soiled, don't fit anymore or you have never worn before. Some drawers may require you to categories items in them so that they don't become mixed up and make it harder to identify. For example, if you're going to be storing your under wears with your socks it is before you have a separate space for your socks so that they don't get lost in the sea of singlets. If the drawers in your bedroom do not come with any demarcations, you can find a way to create some for yourself.

To create more space in your clothes drawer, you can fold them and place them like folders in the drawer. This way you make a smaller mess whenever you pull them out of the drawer.

DEMARCATING THE WORKSPACE FROM A RELAXATION SPACE
It's always advisable that you have a separate workspace that will be fully differentiated from your relaxation space. Peradventure you live in a small house and can't help but work in your bedroom, it's best you have a small demarcation to distinguish both spaces.

Not only do you have to keep the work area tidy, you'll also need to ensure that you don't find yourself returning to work at odd hours. Clutter cuts across various aspects of your life and it can also affect your schedule. This is why you'll need to keep both aspects of your life independent of each other. Don't allow little things like paper clutter outgrow the office space and land on the bed.

To keep the office space as decluttered as possible take note of these:
is there office equipment that may have outgrown their importance?
If you've upgraded to newer models what did you do with the older ones? Are they still lying around in the office space?

There's a high chance that you'll come across such items that should be dealt with appropriately. If you find out that you won't be making use of it then you can give it out as a donation or sell of their parts. A quick hack for your office space is to have a drawer underneath the work desk. This place will be used to store all of the work items that you use occasionally while working.

THE CLOSET

Closets are basically used to store up clothes, shoes and other materials that you have been unable to find space for in the main bedroom. Closets basically function to ensure that clutter doesn't find its way into the bedroom in dorm of scattered clothes and shoes, but closets on their own can become cluttered. Sometimes the closet can become so neglected that you don't notice the dust building up at the back, close to the wall.

The first step to do is to clear off everything sitting on the closet shelves. Clean the shelves thoroughly, brushing off the dust and removing cobwebs hanging on the walls. Begin to sort through the items, selecting those that you will keep and those that will be given away. Do this for every shelf lying in the closet until all the items are well sorted out. Remember to be as truthful to yourself as possible. When you pick up an item, try to ask yourself what role that item has played in your life during the past few months? Are there shoes you haven't used in years? These are some of things that should give way so that your closet comes out in its best.

When returning items back to the closet shelves, there should be some slight rearrangements to produce the best results. For example, more frequently used items should be kept on the lowest shelves where they can easily be reached, especially by the children. Supplies that are kept in the closet should be packed in special containers so that they don't fall off the shelf and spill. Since towels will be wet most of the time, you should find a special compartment for them where they will receive enough natural light and air so that they don't become soggy and pollute the closet with a weird smell. The best option is to take them out of the house until they are dried before they'll be put inside the closet.

Rearranging the clothes in the closet can be quite time consuming, so you might need to sacrifice some of your time for this. You won't just rearrange the same clothing into the closet the same way they were removed. Take out some time to go through the items and select those clothes that will need to go. Also pay attention to off-season clothes like winter coats and gloves. You'll need to store them away from the others so that you can have enough space for those that are used more often. When arranging longer clothes, make sure that the hangers are high enough to prevent their hems from touching the closet floor or other lower racks. Shoes should be taken off the floor and kept on racks.

You'll face other miscellaneous items while decluttering your closet. Pick them up and place them in their appropriate categories. The belts should preferably hang from extension from the walls. Bags that aren't used frequently should be kept on the highest shelves. Sort through these items and organize them into items with functions that most closely resemble each other.

After decluttering your closet for the first time, don't forget to go with the principle of 'one in one out'. If you get a new pair of trousers, don't forget to either give one out or trash it. There has to be a replacement, not mindless additions. There will be a lot of emotional attachments obvious when dealing with your clothes, but you need to be more rigid. There's really need to hang on the fence. If your first impulse to a clothing material is to keep it, then you have to answer the necessary question of 'why'? This will help you stay as objective as possible while making so decisions and provide you with the best results possible.

Using Colors To Your Advantage
Making use of color differences in your closet arrangement is one life hack that will make it easy for you to keep your closet organized. As you return the clothes into the closet, try to study the color pattern of your cloth collection and find out the best way to arrange them for the best effect. You can also do this for your hats, your scarves and your shoes.

THE CHILDREN'S ROOM
When decluttering the children's room, make sure that you actively involve them. Not only will you be helping them live better, but you'll also be teaching them an important live lesson that will change their lives. There are many ways in which you can begin to declutter their lives, and one of such ways is by regulating the number of items for buy for them including toys and clothing. Doing this will help them appreciate the little they have and learn to treat them with respect.

Note that you'll have to treat their room with respect while decluttering. It's their space and you should seek their opinion before making any decision concerning their belonging. So when you walk into the room and discover any dorm of clutter, first tell them about what you're about to do. Then pull out the clutter from the places where they are hiding and make them choose those they would love to keep. The others can be thrown into the donation box to be given out. It might shock you to discover that your children has already been thinking about decluttering for a while but has been waiting for just one push.

After dealing with the toys, you can now face the surfaces, the drawers, the beds and the closets and go through the same procedure as listed above.

A Short Note for Your Footwear
Footwear can become problematic, especially when they aren't treated right. If you're a shoe person, you can have so much that you begin to lose track of your shoe possessions. So there should be a system in your home to deal with the shoe clutter.

The first premise you should know about decluttering shoes is that they should leave the ground. There are a lot of negatives associated with keeping shoes on the ground, some of which include space deprivation and litters of dried sand and dust clogging the floor. Keeping them in their personalized storage spaces can go a long way in keeping them more organized and beautifying your home in the long run. There are a variety of options you can explore for organizing your shoe collections. Some of them include:

- Shoe bags

You can store your shoes in shoe bags and hang them on a wall somewhere in one corner of the room or behind a door. Shoe bags are a wonderful option, especially for the storage of sport shoes. You only have to ensure that you don't put in a wet shoe into the shoe bag because it can ultimately lead to the formation of molds and irritating stench in the bag. Make sure to occasionally take out the shoes for cleaning.

- Shoe Racks

Shoe racks are perfect for more stylish shoes, especially for high-heeled shoes. You can either go for a shoe rack that sits on the floor or one than hangs on a wall. Either way the shoe rack is always a go option because it easily helps you manage your collection. Occasionally dust off the rack to remove cobwebs and dust.

Keeping your bedroom generally decluttered with require a lot of habit change. Without this change, all of your effort will remain useless. You'll have to stay consistent throughout the period of change so that you subconscious begin to adopt these new habits. For instance, you must ensure that your clothes find their way to the closet when you return home and not to dump them on the bed. Books and magazine brought into the room should be returned to the bookshelf as soon as you're through reading. Keeping them on the nightstand doesn't assist you with your decluttering.

CHAPTER SIX: DECLUTTERING THE HOME OFFICE

With the current evolution going on in the world today, more and more people are beginning to embrace and understand the concept of working from home. While it can be very wonderful to work from home, there are some disadvantages associated with it. Some of the disadvantages include the ease with which work and family life can slip into the each other without clear distinctions and the stress of finding the perfect workspace in your home.

To run a successful home-based business, you'll need more than pure grit and business mindedness. Working from home will require you to understand how to manage your time and resources for the best results possible. Selecting a workspace in your home will require a little brainstorming that will help you select either the option of having your workspace in your bedroom or a separate room entirely. In this chapter, we'll explore the available options and how you can create a clutter-free space that will help you stay more productive.

THE MAJOR REQUIREMENT

The best tactic you can do when you start decluttering your office space is to ask yourself necessary questions after making a selection of the perfect space. The question to ask is: 'What will I be doing here?' This question is important because it'll give definition and purpose to your space. Without that clean and clear cut purpose you'll find to hard knowing the major items that you will need in your space. When starting up your office space, there are some equipment you may think you need, but the truth is that you can do without them. This is where extensive planning come into place. Without the foundation of a comprehensive plan, you'll find yourself purchasing random items that will soon result in clutter.

The most important questions you will need to ask yourself before you start decluttering your workspace are:
- What purpose will this space serve? Or: What activities will be performed here?
- Is there equipment with newer, smaller and more functional models I can buy?
- How possible will it be to make the entire connections between equipment to wireless Ones?
- Do I go digital entirely. If no, then how do I plan to hand all my paperwork?
- How about your area for storing office supplies? What method of classification will you be using?

There are some other questions that can be asked and they all depend on the arrangement you chose to use in your office space. The questions will majorly stem from the arrangement system you chose to use and some other basic factors affecting your personal workspace.

STARTING UP THE PROCESS
Like I noted earlier, decluttering the workspace will require a lot if input so as to produce the best quality. It isn't just as about making rearrangements to the already existing space. There are some necessary steps you will need to undertake to achieve success with the decluttering process. It's standard, the same as the other parts of the home.

First, you must identify the major points of clutter accumulation and begin to take away everything that seems to constitute a clutter in that space. It can be the shelves for storing paperwork, or the drawer directly underneath the work desk. Whatever it is, be vigilant to take out everything occupying those cluttered spaces. If you're going to be multi-purposing one room to serve the functions of workspace and another, then there will need to have a clear cut demarcation between the two spaces to avoid mixtures.

THE PAPER CLUTTER
In the most prominent causative of office clutter is paper, paper and more paper. Even with the current 'digitalization' of the business world, it's still hard to do without them. You best bet is knowing how to handle them. There are always piles of them waiting around to be addressed and sorted. Pick the largest pile and start up work.

You'll basically have to go through each of those receipts, documents, flyers and scripts. Scan through and select those that might still be important to you in the near future. Note that you will come across a lot of interesting information from your past that will make you stop and linger over the nostalgia associated with your past. This is not the time to start looking at vacation pictures or rereading magazine articles. You need to be as fast as possible. If the paper isn't important, then it isn't life or death. There is no need saving it for the future. If you haven't needed it in year, you might never require it again.

When you come across documents that you need, make a classification system that makes it easier for you to find them in the future. The major categories that papers in your office will fall into any of the following: receipts, paid bills, bank statements, investment records, insurance information, and other categories might make their way into your list. It all depends on the kinds of documents that you deal with in your office space. The beauty of it is that you now have a wonderful classification that makes it easier to find your documents instead a messy pile that frustrates you.

THE OFFICE DESK

The office desk is a workspace, and like every other functional workspace, it's supposed to have enough space to provide you the best comfort possible.

The first tip to note is that the office space is to contain only those things you make use of on a daily basis. This will include your computer system, a notebook, a pen, etc. Everything else should be put into a drawer and hidden away until it is needed. The ideal decluttered desk space is one that allows you sit on your bench and stretch your arm as far as possible on the workspace without any form of hindrance. You can have some of your personal belongings on the table, such as some family photos, but you should also know where to draw the line, so that it doesn't become too jam-packed.

After you have successfully created these categories, you'll now be able to know how many drawers would be needed to correctly file them. You can place two or three of these folders in one drawer, depending on their size and contents. The folders containing a category of papers that you rarely use should be placed in the drawer farthest from you. Folders that you'll refer to more often should be in the drawers closer to you.

On the desk surface, you'll have the files to refer to as least one every hour. These are everyday files that contain crucial information for the smooth running of your business. You can make use of a folder rack to store these folders. It helps you save space and prevent a pile up of folder again. Also, with a folder rack, it's easier to sort through your folders. But be careful not to overload the rack with folders and more folders. The weight of the combined folders is enough to cause a breakage at the bottom on the rack and damage it.

THE BEST HABITS TO ADOPT TO PREVENT THE RE-ACCUMULATION OF PAPER CLUTTER

- **The Bills**

The most important note to make here is when you pay your bills since timing is imperative. It varies between individuals, but you should have a short note on when you intend to pay your bills.

If you're the kind of person who forgets the bills until they accumulate, you can subscribe to an automatic payment method. This will help you settle your bills even without knowing it. Others ways are by placing bill settlement in the hands of a family member who's very organized and good with finances or handling it over to a book keeper or a financial organization.

The best way to deal with incoming paperwork is to have a standard system that works. Before now, you may not have had a system in place for dealing with paperwork. You'll need to create one now. It's a simple procedure and I'll provide you with actionable guidelines to help you through the process. Follow these tips:

- The first to do with papers as they arrive is to send them into the category where they best fit. This should be an easy task that can be carried out at least once every day. The main thing here is to ensure that every paper that has come in for the day is given a new home before that day ends. It doesn't mean that you deal with all the papers in one day, but you have at least made the work easier and decluttered the space for incoming paper.
- Each category and paper classification has a specific action attached to it. For the bills, all must be paid. Letters need to be replied to swiftly. Questionnaires should be answered and sent back. All of these are the actions related to these papers. This way, when you decide to work on the papers in one category, you already know what you want to achieve.
- If you deal with a lot of papers in your workspace, then a larger portion of the space should be dedicated to the storage and filing of these papers, especially when it is obvious that the table space will never be enough to contain all of those. The major factor that will determine the space to designate for paperwork will depend on much of such you handle per day.
- Finally, in your paper space, there should also be a provision for paperwork containing **Maintain contractions here** relevant task records, so that it'll be easy to find them when need arises.

THE SCANNING OPTION

In the previous section, we've discussed extensively on how you can handle paper clutter, but the question is: Won't you love to get rid of them if you truly can? Won't it be wonderful to have your life digitalized instead of choked up with paperwork? The answer is 'yes' and I tell you that is a quick solution for that. You can scan you documents with a digital scanner to be reproduced or printed on a later date.

Scanning is a great option for reducing paperwork, but you have to know that not all of your documents should be scanned. Also, some can be scanned but their originals should be kept no matter what. Some papers are best presented in their physical copies, such as certificates and sealed documents. When you scan, start with documents without seals or other less important documents such as receipts, prove of payments, etc. After settling those, you can now go ahead and scan the more important ones.

Finally, you'll need to save your scanned documents to a storage cloud for easy retrieval. It can be iCloud, Dropbox or Google Drive. Wherever you decided to use, just make sure that you have the password written out somewhere safe, a place you can return to and retrieve it when needed. Also, you can ask your financial institution or companies you buy from if they provide online statements. Online statements make it easier because they can be downloaded anytime and referred to repeatedly.

HANDLING THE DIGITAL CLUTTER IN YOUR WORKSPACE

The digital aspect of world is ever evolving. Each day, more apps, software and computer programs are being introduced to help make life easier for us. Because of this, studying digital clutter can be broader than it seems. One method can work for you today, but within three months' time, it may become obsolete, so you must need to learn to move with the time.

In this section, we'll briefly consider the ways in which we can manage digital clutter and stay ahead in our digital lives.

Most of the stuff in our digital lives exists basically in your computer system, so that is going to be our focus: organizing the computer system. Here are some basic tips that will help you to achieve these goals:

- There has to be a central point for the storage of your files. This means that your digital files should be arranged in such a way that a stranger than easily assess your file location simply by receiving mere directions from you. For some people, it has gotten so bad that they can't even find digital files in their own computer system. You don't know how disastrous that can be, especially when you think you must have deleted a file but can't find it in the recycle bin and you have forgotten the name of the file. With a centralized and we'll organized system, you will be able to find the needed file with a quick scan.
- After achieving a centralized system, you must establish an actionable procedure that will help you with the storage of your file. The best method of file classification is according to contents. It's always easier to find them this way.
  For instance, if you're going to be storing some photographs of you with the baby lying on a beach in a vacation on some Thailand beach, here's what you can do: My photos > Family photos > Vacation photos > Thailand > At the beach. With this comprehensive breakdown, there will be no way you won't be able to easily identity file locations when you need them.
- If you notice that the files on your system are beginning to pile up into a clutter, you can upload them into a cloud storage to create more space in your computer. There are a lot of online storage options open to you such as Dropbox, Microsoft One Drive, Cloud Me, etc. All you will need to do is make a little research on all of them and find the one that suits you best.

- Digital Clutter also extends to the time we spend online, on social media platforms. How do you manage your time online? Do you spend hours watching Instagram skits or scrolling through meme pages? Yes, a little fun doesn't hurt anybody, but at some point you become obsessed and lose track of the valuable things. Remember that this is the opposite of minimalism and decluttering. These two help you to identify the most important valuables in your life, instead. There should be a regulation that helps get you back on track once your fun time has elapsed so that you get back to being productive.
- Emails should be handled as urgently as possible. Don't allow them pile up in your email box and overwhelm you. It's almost impossible to clear up all the emails in your inbox daily, but you should have a target for each day. At least you can decide to handle and reply 20 emails per day. This way you reduce the workload over a period of time. Also, you must set aside a specific period during the day when you reply to emails. It shouldn't be something you just start doing out of the blue.
- Keep the items on your desktop to the barest minimum so that only the most important folders and files can be found on it. It makes no sense to have your desktop filled with folders and files. You can make the work easier for yourself by grouping like contents into one main folder.
- Uninstall software you no longer need. Go through the program list on your system and delete packages that you rarely use. A system packed with heavy and unused software will definitely lag.
- To control the quantity of emails you receive, thoroughly scan through your inbox and find irrelevant subscriptions you may have made in the past and unsubscribe from them.
- Occasionally delete duplicated photos and files in your system.
- Make use of a password manager that helps you control your passwords so that even when they're forgotten, they can be retrieved from that manager.
- Whenever you want to embark on a serious task, put your phone on silent mode or switch it off entirely so you can concentrate.

ELECTRONICS AND CABLES

You'll always have and need electronics in your workspace, so you should be able to look out for them to prevent them from taking over your workspace. You will have to take extra care when making a decision to buy a new electronic gadget. What if you can pay a little amount and get the same job done for you without owning the equipment? For example, photocopying. Getting one covers a lot of space in your office, but this is something you can quickly do outside for a small amount, or ask a neighbor so you can quickly use theirs.

Dusty gadgets are repulsive. They hinder you from working as fast as you need to; plus, they're more susceptible to damage once they are clogged up with dust in their inner components. Because of this, it's necessary that you dust your gadgets occasionally to prevent an accumulation. Take time to inspect the smaller spaces in these gadgets and find places where dust gathers the most. If possible, cover them up with a light material to prevent the entrance of dust.

CHAPTER SEVEN: DECLUTTERING YOUR SCHEDULE

Decluttering, as I have started earlier, encompasses various aspects of our lives. Most people have become so consumed with the need to declutter their homes of physical stuff that they forget that other parts of their lives need to be decluttered. Your schedule is one of those aspects; and once you miss it, it affects other facets of your life. A clear and organized schedule for each day is an immense blessing. It gives you a clearer vision and helps you maximize your time and your day. This is why you'll need to understand how to maximize your schedule to the fullest.

Here are some of the ways in which you can begin to effectively declutter your schedule:

1. Saying no and meaning it

Every one of us is blessed with the same number of hours per day. The beautiful part about it is that people around us are knowingly or unknowingly looking to steal some of our hours per day. It's now left to you to allow them succeed or not.

You can't be everywhere at the same time, neither can you do numerous things are the same instant. But this won't stop the commitments from presenting themselves. It's at this point that you'll need to draw out a scale of preference. It's this drawn out scale of preference that will assist you to sieve out and allow only the important activities to exist in your schedule.

Saying no to the wrong things will ultimately help you say yes to the right things. This will means that you have more space and time to achieve better results and your time is spent doing more productive things. So each day, wake up with a mindset to declutter your schedule. Make a list of all the place you need to go and things you need to do. Go through the list one more time and I bet you'll find some activities that you can scribble off, to be performed on a later date or to be assigned to someone else.

2. Set your priorities right

The truth is that even after scribbling off things from your list you'll still have a lot to do. It's only natural. This is all for the sake of productivity. So this is where you will need to make your priorities. What do you need to do before the other? Say you wake up one morning and you have a bunch of Emails to address. Sending those replies is very critical, but you'll need to set aside enough time to do it. Let's say you ignore the kids and begin to reply those mails by 6:40 AM, while the kids roam the house aimlessly with no one to supervise them to prepare for school. That's a perfect scenario depicting a recipe for disaster. The first thing to do would've been to get the kids to school first then settle down and reply those mails.

Setting your priority helps to provide you with an action plan. Instead of you going through the day without and aim, unsure of what to expect, you find yourself better prepared with each rising sun, set to complete each task as they present themselves.

Setting your priority means making a list and ranking them from most important to least important. This can sometimes be a daunting task, but you'll need to perform it if you want to achieve any form of decluttering in your schedule. Selecting the activities that will rank higher than other depends solely on you. For one person, replying to email is more vital that visiting the grocery store. For another person it's the other way round. So you'll need to have a deep understanding of your schedule if you want make a priority ranking.

3. **Review your schedule**

You must have heard it said over and over again: time is money, but you can't understand how powerful and true that sentence is, even in its short length. Most times people just tend to run into conclusions that the reason they are unable to complete certain tasks within a given period of time is simply because they don't have enough time. For every task that you cannot complete within a given period of time, there's somebody somewhere fulfilling that same task within that period. The question is how they do it?

People who achieve the most are people who have learnt to review their schedule until it is near perfect. Schedule review helps you to remove the fat until you find the real gem. In reviewing you schedule. you should ask yourself one important question whenever you come across an activity: What value does completing this activity add to my life? Please be as subjective as possible when providing as answer. Answering this question will help you identify the ideals of your life.

Any activity that fails this test is definitely not a value adding one. You'll need to scrap it. Employ ruthlessness while doing this so that sentiment doesn't blind you. What are the excesses lurking around your schedule. Do you really need to spend one hour each day watching cat videos in YouTube? Would the world come to an end if you spend more time reading a motivational book instead of scrolling through Netflix? You need to find out that the answers to these questions is 'no;' and once the resolutions are implemented, there will be a change. This is where discipline and focus comes in place. Once the excesses in your schedule are cleared off, never go back to your toxic lifestyle, no matter how tempted you may be.

4. **Assign tasks**

In completing your daily tasks and activities, you'll encounter some stumbling blocks along the way. Sometimes, no matter how much you try to declutter your schedule and stay more productive, you'll still discover that completing all of those tasks will seem almost impossible. Being able to successfully combine the different aspects of your life, including family life and work is always very stressful. At this point you'll need to understand that you cannot do it alone. You'll have to delegate tasks to get things done as quickly as possible.

Delegating tasks to different people is a particularly effective trick that you can use especially in an office setting where you have staff working under you. If you find out that you always fall behind your schedule because you have more than enough to achieve within a short period of time, then you should consider getting more hands on board. Make a list of tasks that need to be completed and select those that too sensitive to be given to some else. You can handle those ones yourself. Other non-time sensitive ones can be handled by a competent member of your workforce.

One major benefit you stand to enjoy when you delegate tasks is that it helps you prepare them for future tasks of that nature. But note that it isn't as easy as it seems. You'll need to do better that just delegate a task. You must be very watchful and observant, to be teacher ready to correct a student over and over as they work. If you leave them unsupervised, you might come back to a disaster.

You can also bring the delegating spirit home and practice with the kids. No matter how small they are, there are little tasks that you can assign to them. The smallest ones can do little things like take the boots and foot wears to their designated spaces. Initially, you may need to supervise some of them on those tasks, but as time goes on they become more comfortable completing those tasks in your absence.

5. Break free from perfectionism!

Beholding something so perfect can sometimes be described as a heavenly blessing. Some people are just wired to take it as long as it is ok and meets basic standards. Others are programmed with a different kind of DNA that won't accept anything until it is 110% perfection. At some point, being the perfectionist in the room kind of sets you apart and helps you excel. But the older and more matured you become, you'll come to understand that nothing is ever perfect. Everything comes with its own sets of identifiable flaws.

Nothing kills your time more than yearning for perfection. Nothing is ever perfect, but a stage of good enough can be achieved. Perfectionism kills time and prevents you from performing other tasks that need to be performed. You'll continuously discover faults that no one else cares about and this is time consuming. All you will have to is to ensure that you've personally put in your best effort into each task them gradually move on the next task on your list.

Also, don't expect perfectionism from people you have delegated tasks to generally. They might not be perfectionists like you, and it's best to appreciate the little effort they have put in so that you can lift up their spirits to do more next time. You can make a few corrections here and there, but do not dwell on their mistakes and chide them over the work done. Immediately you've able to get over the perfectionist mindset, you'll be amazed at the quantity and quality of things you can easily scribble off from your schedule.

CONCLUSION

The journey to minimalism and decluttering is a never-ending journey. Moreover, it's a gradually process that will help you arrive at a greater good if you keep at it for long enough. There are different reasons why people embark on the minimalism journey, all of which are valid at any given point in time. It's my sincere hope that this book has done enough you with enough equipment that will guide through your adventurous journey through minimalism.

The beauty about reading books like this is in taking actions immediately. One person said that ideas rule the world. I beg to differ. I think that ideas with corresponding actions rule the world. If you've read this book without taking the necessary action listed throughout it, then you've achieved nothing. Reading this book only once is never enough. It should serve as a guide that you can return to over and over until you've fully acclimatized yourself with everything taught in it.

In reality you'll likely encounter a lot of things while on your journey through minimalism. You might be tempted over and over to return to your consumerism mindset and forfeit all you have worked hard to achieve. Don't fall into that trap. You'll regret it after on. In earlier chapters, I listed out some ways in which you can overcome this urge. You might also encounter people who will make conscious efforts to tear down your efforts and bring you down to their state. They may look down on you for not spending as much as they do and not living as flamboyantly and they do. But you have to remember that the value of life isn't in the quantity of your possessions but in their quality. If you take only one thing from this book, it's that less is always more, no matter how ironic it may sound.

One of the greatest keys to succeeding at a minimalist is by surrounding yourself with people of your tribe, people that think just like you. Find other minimalists like you and engage them in friendship. Follow relevant decluttering and minimalism pages on Facebook, Instagram, and other social media platforms. This way you are constantly reminded about the importance of minimalism. There's more information and support on the internet than you need. Seek them so that they can provide you with the motivation needed to carry on with this life changing process.

Finally, you'll need to be a minimalism champion. Talk to people about the concept until you're able to convince them. It's beautiful when you live your life as a minimalist, but it is definitely more beautiful when everyone around you is an active minimalist. Start from within, your children and your spouse. Then stretch further and talk to the neighbors, depending on how close you are to them. Outline the benefits and make their mouths water. You can even bring them into your home and show them proof of the benefits. You'll come across strong-headed people unwilling to yield. You'll also meet people who will be willing to give it a try. These are the people you need to show as much support as possible. They'll comprise your decluttering support system and vice versa!

Printed in Great Britain
by Amazon